FIRST MEDICINE MAN

FIRST MEDICINE MAN
THE TALE OF
YOBAGHU-TALYONUNH

by
ARTHUR R. WRIGHT

Illustrations by
BILL ENGLES

Afterword by
JOAN E. WEIS

O. W. FROST, Publisher
Anchorage, Alaska
1977

Copyright, 1977, by O. W. Frost

The tale in this book was first printed in the *Alaskan Churchman* between 1926 and 1930. It is here published in book form for the first time.

Library of Congress Card Number 77-99137
International Standard Book Number 0-930766-03-2 Cloth Edition
International Standard Book Number 0-930766-04-0 Paperback Edition

Manufactured in the United States of America
Printed and bound by The Caxton Printers, Ltd.
Caldwell, Idaho 83605
131931

CONTENTS

FOREWORD

THIS is the tale of Yobaghu-Talyonunh (Ya-bog Tal-yawn-a) as it is told during the long winter nights when the old man of the village feels disposed to entertain. It is a tale hardly known nowadays by the youth of the tribes, who do not have much interest in it. But it is a story that has been handed down by word of mouth from generation to generation, told by the elders with the object of passing on to their successors the customs of the tribes and to explain many things — the natures of different animals, how the canoe is made, the snowshoe fashioned; why the silver-tip is dreaded, the wolverine outlawed. While the tale is not the same among all the tribes, it is told of the same hero among all the Indians of Alaska.

Yobaghu-Talyonunh was the first medicine man, and a good one. All that he did was in the interest and welfare of man. With but a few exceptions, he subdued all creatures to his will and those exceptions would have been overcome but for some trickery or conspiracy of the elements. Much of what follows is strange and cannot be explained, but what has been possible to piece together is given here.

Arthur R. Wright

FIRST MEDICINE MAN

1.

YOBAGHU-TALYONUNH AND HIS TWO WIVES

YOBAGHU-TALYONUNH had two wives. The older one did not treat him well. One day he asked her for a drink of water and she gave him some that was not clean. Yobaghu-Talyonunh took it and drank it, saying nothing. But the next morning he disappeared, and his wives knew that something was wrong because he said nothing before leaving.

Worrying about what he might do, the older one followed. That was just what he had not wished. He was going on a long journey to seek adventure and he did not want the burden of his family.

So, after going for some distance he said to himself, "I wish I would see a great wolf." And presently a wolf appeared.

Yobaghu-Talyonunh slew it, and propping it into as natural a position as he could and prying its jaws apart with sticks to make it look fierce, he left it in his trail. In like manner he killed a bear and placed it in the trail. For a long distance along the way, he left many ferocious looking animals apparently waiting to attack anyone who should come that way.

When the older wife came upon these creatures, she was frightened and ran back. She told the other wife what she had seen.

"Why did you not make a noise and see if they would move? Why were you afraid?" the younger woman asked.

"Well, then you go!" retorted the older woman, angrily.

The younger wife started out, carrying her baby on her back. She walked until she came to the wolf. She threw sticks at him, and when he did not move she knew that he was dead. She had known her husband's mind better than the other!

For two days and nights she followed her husband's trail. In her anxiety to catch up with him, she forgot to care for the baby or even to stop for food for herself. It was cold weather, and when she reached her husband's camp, the child was dead.

Yobaghu-Talyonunh was a man of few words but much thought. He said nothing when he saw his second wife, but offered her the care he was accustomed to give her, and the next day they traveled together.

2.

TAILS OF THE WOLVES

THEY came one day to a great lake, and on the other side they saw two wolves squatted on their haunches, watching. Yobaghu-Talyonunh made a high cache for his wife to hide in, and then he built a wall of trees. He advanced toward the wolves, and as one started to charge him, he ran back, jumped upon his wall, and as the wolf followed him, he hit the wolf with a club, killing it. He repeated the trick with the second wolf.

Wolves have never since attempted to kill man.

Yobaghu-Talyonunh took the tails of the wolves and stuck them in his hat, telling his wife to watch for the tails. If they disappeared she would know that he was dead.

Now it was a custom as a show of respect and good will to a guest to shout and toss him into the air on the shoulders. Thus Yobaghu-Talyonunh's wife could easily distinguish him from others.

He started for the village that was on the other side of the lake, and as his wife watched she saw the people rush toward him and toss him into the air. She would see the tails disappear for a time and she would begin to weep, but when she would see the tails she was glad.

3.

THE TAIL-MAN AND HIS CHILDREN

THE FOX made friends with Yobaghu-Talyonunh and invited him into a hut for a meal. As he ate, Yobaghu-Talyonunh put pieces away for his wife. The Fox noticed and asked him in a whisper if he had a wife, adding the warning that the Tail-man was no good and to watch him.

Despite their caution the Tail-man overheard, and he at once went out to the lake and began to shout, "Someone's wife is out here!"

Whereupon all the men ran out.

Then the Fox exclaimed, "Oh, my friend!" and followed the rest.

Yobaghu-Talyonunh knew that he could not save his wife, so he prepared to get his revenge. With a burning log from the fire, he branded and beat all the women of the camp except the fox-woman.

Since then, all the animal people have hated and feared man.

Meanwhile, the Tail-man climbed the cache and was about to seize Yobaghu-Talyonunh's wife and claim her as his captive when the Fox grabbed him and threw him off. Then the Fox took

Yobaghu-Talyonunh's wife and brought her to her husband.

The Fox and Yobaghu-Talyonunh became even greater friends.

The next day the camp was moved. Now, in moving camp, the men always went ahead, the women coming behind and pulling the sleds.

It happened that Yobaghu-Talyonunh's wife was the last woman in the train.

The Tail-man hid beside the trail until all had passed, and then he made advances to Yobaghu-Talyonunh's wife. She refused to talk to him, whereupon he grew angry and slew her.

When the men reached the camping place, the Tail-man boasted that he had killed someone's wife.

Yobaghu-Talyonunh waited for some time, and when his wife did not appear he thought, "He must speak true." He was very sorry.

One day when the men were having a shooting match with bows and arrows, Yobaghu-Talyonunh deliberately shot the Tail-man. As fast as they could, he and the Fox began to chop the Tail-man to pieces. When they came to the end of the tail, it bounced up and away.

Yobaghu-Talyonunh did not take much notice of this, but the Fox said, "You do not know the Tail-man!"

When Yobaghu-Talyonunh and the Fox returned to the camp, the children of the Tail-man were singing, "Before the dawn brightens the sky, our father will return."

Sure enough, in the morning the Tail-man walked into camp still singing his song that he had killed someone's wife.

Yobaghu-Talyonunh was very much surprised and mystified. But after much thought he decided that the secret lay in the tail of the Tail-man.

So at their next shooting match when he again shot the Tail-man, he and the Fox chopped him up as before. But when they came to the tail, Yobaghu-Talyonunh caught it and held the end tightly in his hand.

The tail spoke, "This is the end. I am helpless now."

Yobaghu-Talyonunh and the Fox piled trees over the Tail-man, taking pains to weight the end of the tail down firmly. Then they covered the heap mountain-high with snow.

When they went back to the camp, the children of the Tail-man were singing as before, "Before the dawn brightens the sky, our father will return."

"No, this is the end of your father," said Yobaghu-Talyonunh.

All night, scratchings were heard and a voice said, "My children, I can help it no longer. I can never return."

To this day, many people quiet their children at night by making scatching noises on the floor or wall and saying, "The spirit of the Tail-man is at work!"

The next morning all the Tail-children (who were the weasel, the mink, the lynx, and such) went to the heap of trees and ice that had formed into a mountain, and they built a fire to thaw it out.

But they could do nothing, for their father cried, "It is hot! It is hot!" When they tried to chop him out, he cried, "Aba! Aba!" which means "Ouch!"

There are some that think the Tail-children are still trying to thaw their father out, for to this day the mountain smokes at intervals, and often great rumblings are heard inside. These are said to be the rumblings of the Tail-man at his bad luck.

4.

FISH-HAWK

AFTER the death of his wife, Yobaghu-Talyonunh traveled alone. One day he saw on each side of the trail a mark, as if someone had thrown a dog whip from side to side. Soon he saw a fire ahead. Upon reaching the fire, he saw a Fish-hawk man who invited him to sit down.

The Fish-hawk immediately removed the fish roasting by the fire. He very carefully cleaned and picked out the bones, leaving only the tempting white meat.

Yobaghu-Talyonunh was very hungry. He thought the Fish-hawk was eating all the fish, because he couldn't see from where he was sitting just what the Fish-hawk was doing. So he very stealthily took out his little horn club and was going to knock the Fish-hawk on the head when the Fish-hawk turned with the plate of clean fish and said, "Here, my friend. I didn't want you to swallow any bones."

Yobaghu-Talyonunh ate as much as he could. What was left he cached among some spruce boughs. Chance might bring him back this way, and he would know that he had a cache if he were hungry.

The next day they started out, the Fish-hawk leading the way. As he went, he tossed his fishline from side to side, but he caught nothing. Finally, he said: "My friend, did you by any chance leave some of your fish behind? If so, please go back, find it, and eat it before you come on. I'll make camp and wait for you."

Yobaghu-Talyonunh went back and did as the Fish-hawk requested. When he returned, the Fish-hawk explained that they never left any food nor wasted any. He had cleaned out the bones so that he could eat them himself. If he wasted any part, he would be hungry.

He threw out his line again. This time he brought out fish from under the ice, and they had plenty to eat.

So it was that Yobaghu-Talyonunh discovered that fish was good to eat, and he devised means of his own for obtaining them.

In olden times the Indians used the cambrium layer of the willow and alder which they shreaded and made into twine. These they knit into dip nets, to be used with long spruce handles.

5.

WOLVERINE

AFTER "two sleeps," Yobaghu-Talyonunh left the Fish-hawk and traveled alone again. It was evening when he found himself on a very wide flat with no timber to make camp. In the distance he could see a faint light. He went towards it and soon came to the camp of a Wolverine.

The Wolverine man lay full length by the fire. He greeted Yobaghu-Talyonunh and asked where he was going in such an out of the way place. He then feigned great weariness and told Yobaghu-Talyonunh to make himself comfortable and to help himself from the provisions.

Yobaghu-Talyonunh did so and brought to the firelight a large skin of moose fat.

The Indians render their fats from the animals they kill and put them into the stomachs and bladders of their kill. These are cached against hard times.

Yobaghu-Talyonunh recognized something very familiar about this particular skin, and said to the Wolverine that he thought he had placed it in his own cache last fall. He wondered how the Wolverine had come by it.

The Wolverine is one of the most thieving and trickiest of animals.

The Wolverine by this time became very much embarrassed and would not speak to his guest. He turned his back to the fire and remained so until Yobaghu-Talyonunh fell asleep.

Before daylight came, Yobaghu-Talyonunh felt cold and, opening his eyes, found that he was alone in the flat with not a tree in sight, nor any sign of the camp. It was snowing heavily.

The camp had been the Wolverine's tail, and a very convenient camp it was since it could be carried easily and placed into position when needed without any trouble.

6.

THE BEGINNING OF MEDICINE MAKING

YOBAGHU-TALYONUNH started on again. He traveled for a long time through a wasted and barren country, and he became very hungry.

It was during this period of his travels that he had time to consider many things, especially the ways of the animal folk. He believed they had mysterious power which helped them gain their livelihood. Had not the Fish-hawk mysteriously pulled fish from the trail at will? Had not the Wolverine covered his tracks by willing it to snow? Why could not he acquire the same power of willing things to be? Why?

With these thoughts, he plodded through the snow, getting weaker and weaker from hunger. He concentrated on his plight. He kept saying to himself, "If I do not eat, I will die."

Suddenly, a voice said, "Yobaghu-Talyonunh, what is that I see following behind you? Uho! Uho! Uho!" This exclamation has to do with mysterious communications in medicine making.

Turning around quickly, Yobaghu-Talyonunh saw in the distance two moose crossing his trail. Stringing his bow, he waited until the moose passed him. Then he killed them both. He was saved from starvation.

Thus did Yobaghu-Talyonunh come to believe that he could commune with the spirit world and get help in times of dire necessity.

He resolved to make use of this power from

then on. This power was the beginning of medicine making.

He dressed the moose, which were exceedingly fat, made camp, and remained there several days.

While he was in camp resting, he saw coming, from opposite directions, two travelers — each coming toward his camp. Both seemed very much spent. On their coming nearer, he recognized his two acquaintances, the Fish-hawk man and the Wolverine man. Both had a sad tale of no food, saying they were very hungry.

Yobaghu-Talyonunh fed them sumptuously and treated them as guests should be treated.

As they were eating, he thought about the limitations of the animal people's minds and about how man, if he willed to, could completely dominate them with his stronger mind. He thought that he could also communicate with, and obtain help from, the supernatural powers when he was in need of food. He had robbed the Fish-hawk man and some others of their power, and they, finding him superior to them, were now coming to him for help.

From then on, the animal people began to fear man more and more.

For several days the Fish-hawk and the Wolverine stayed with Yobaghu-Talyonunh. When the moose meat was almost gone, they each took a pack and started in different directions.

7.

THE LIGHT IN THE MAN'S EYE

IT was still wintertime. After Yobaghu-Talyonunh had traveled some distance, he saw ahead of him a mound of ice and snow. On it there were sharp pointed bones very cunningly concealed so that anyone passing and slipping accidentally would fall and be badly injured. He wondered who could be using these to catch game. He thought he would wait awhile, and, thrusting one of the sharp points through his coat, he pretended to be dead.

The Wolverine pinched him to make sure that his victim was dead. Yobaghu-Talyonunh never moved. Then the Wolverine tied his hands and feet and slung him up and carried him off to camp.

The Wolverine laid Yobaghu-Talyonunh before the fire.

By carefully opening one eye, Yobaghu-Talyonunh could see that the Wolverine had quite a large family.

Yobaghu-Talyonunh now used his newly acquired powers. He wished that his hands and feet might be untied. Soon the Wolverine came over and untied them.

Then he noticed a knife very near his hand. He

very carefully worked it over to his side and pushed it under him.

The mother and father wolverine began to quarrel about the lost knife.

In the meantime one of the little ones on the other side of the fire kept watching Yobaghu-Talyonunh. He noticed Yobaghu-Talyonunh's eyelids flicker and saw that the firelight was reflected in his eye.

"My father, what is that light I see there, right in the man's eye?" shouted the child.

The Wolverine, being already very much irritated and tired, told the little fellow to shut up and hit him with a stick.

Yobaghu-Talyonunh saw his chance, and, jumping up, killed the family except the oldest girl who fled into the woods and climbed a tree.

Yobaghu-Talyonunh went after her and tried to shoot her with his arrows. But through the mysterious power that is attributed to the Wolverine, the arrows fell to the ground without harming her.

Yobaghu-Talyonunh tried fire, but he failed with it also. So he cursed her and said, "May you and your children continue to steal men's caches, so that men may hate you and seek your destruction."

To this day the Wolverine is the most despised of animals.

8.

CAMP ROBBER AND WOODPECKER

THE next day Yobaghu-Talyonunh heard a great noise in the woods. Going to see what it was, he saw a Camp Robber and Woodpecker having a fight.

"I have to work for my grub," said the Woodpecker. "But you steal men's caches."

The Camp Robber became more angry, and pushed the Woodpecker backward into the fire, burning his tail. That is why the Woodpecker now has no tail.

The woodpecker grabbed the Camp Robber by the head and shoved his face into the ashes. That is why the Camp Robber still has the white ashes around his mouth.

Yobaghu-Talyonunh walked up to them and told them not to fight. They immediately made peace and brought him something to eat.

The Woodpecker brought worms. Yobaghu-Talyonunh did not wish to hurt the Woodpecker's feelings, so he carefully slipped the worms into the front of his shirt.

The Camp Robber brought pieces of fat, meat,

and berries. Yobaghu-Talyonunh made a good meal from them.

Then Yobaghu-Talyonunh left this camp, continuing his way around the horizon.

9.

OWL

HE walked some distance and sat down to rest. He saw about him, in the trees, numerous snares made of willow and wondered who could have made them.

He took off his clothes and stuffed them full of grass, putting a strip of fat down the breast of his mummy. He then struck the head through one of the snares and hid nearby to watch.

Soon he heard someone coming, and, looking around, he saw an Owl man.

When the Owl saw what he had in his snare, he began to chuckle to himself. Seizing a short stubby knife from his belt, he went up to the mummy and cut into the breast to see how fat his catch was.

Yobaghu-Talyonunh was so surprised and disgusted that an Owl should gloat over a human victim that he killed the Owl.

Ever since, owls have had great respect for man.

10.

SCREECH OWL

THE winter was over now, the water was running in the creeks, and the larger streams would soon be opened.

Yobaghu-Talyonunh was still traversing the horizon.

He had not come to any camp for a long time, when to his relief he saw ahead of him an old woman sitting on a fishing fence.

He went up to her and she turned her head and looked at him absentmindedly and said nothing.

Yobaghu-Talyonunh knew her to be a Screech Owl woman, the silliest and most absentminded of all birds.

The sun was shining brightly. Yobaghu-Talyonunh took some water and splashed it upon her. She screeched and laughed and twisted her head this way and that and said, "There are no clouds in the sky. Where is the rain coming from?"

Yobaghu-Talyonunh went up to the Screech Owl woman's house, and saw lots of fish cooking by the fire, all of which he took. Some he ate and the rest he hid to see what she would say when she returned. He then sat down and waited for her to come in.

When the Screech Owl came in she said, "Where is my fish? Oh! I must have eaten it all up," and she set to work to prepare some more fish.

Finally, Yobaghu-Talyonunh asked her how far it was to the next camp.

"Not very far down," was all she said.

11.

THE FLY AND THE ANTS

YOBAGHU-TALYONUNH started on, and as he entered the woods he saw on a broken stump something that looked like a horsefly, but it did not seem to have a mouth. As it sat on the stump it would puff out its cheeks. Yobaghu-Talyonunh, looking closely, could see it had no mouth, so he took out his little knife and made a slit where the mouth should be and immediately the Fly cried, "Ha, ha, ha! You have made me a mouth," and flew away.

As Yobaghu-Talyonunh was standing there thinking about how he had helped the Fly, he heard singing in the distance. Following the direction of the singing, he came nearer and nearer to the voices but could see no one.

He sat down on a log. Soon at his feet appeared a tiny dish with half a blueberry on it and tiny pieces of fat. More and more came until finally there was enough before him for a good meal, which he ate.

On either side of the log which he sat on were many holes. Kicking the log, he discovered that it was an ant colony and that the ants had fed him.

These people could not converse with him as the others did. They were such small folks that he could not hear their voices.

<h1 style="text-align:center">12.</h1>

MAKING THE FIRST CANOE

IT was summertime, and Yobaghu-Talyonunh had reached the bank of a great river. It was in line with his travel, and he wished to follow it.

He killed a grouse. As he was eating it, he wondered how he could make something to travel on the water with. The breast bone of the grouse suggested the bow and stern of a canoe, and it was from this that he modeled the first canoe.

He figured out the skeleton for his canoe, and then he started to wonder what he could cover it with. He took pieces of bark from the various trees and tried them by floating them and seeing how far they would go without sinking. The birch bark was the only one which went on and on without sinking, so he decided to cover his frame with birch bark.

Then he began to wonder how the seam should be sewn. He called on the different animals to come and try, but their work did not suit him.

He called again, and four spirits of water in the forms of women came out and showed him the stitch which is still used in sewing up birch canoes.

The women were very beautiful, and he desired one for his wife. He jumped up and caught one of them as they were sliding back into the water, but she bit him and he let her go.

The first three disappeared quickly, but the last one swam angrily about near the surface of the water for some time, washing away the scent of man.

These creatures have never been seen since, but medicine men are able to communicate with them.

Yobaghu-Talyonunh must next find something to stop the seams so they would not leak. He tried the fats of all the different animals and pure pitch, but none would do. Finally, he discovered that by mixing pitch with fat the desired result was produced.

13.

OTTER

HE started downstream. He had not gone very far when he was suddenly aware of a camp. Making a landing, he was told by a Mouse woman that nearby lived an Otter woman who was very bad and would kill human beings.

Now, the Otter woman is descended from the Tail-man, who was destroyed by Yobaghu-Talyonunh. Naturally the Otter woman would be very hostile and cunning in her hostility.

Yobaghu-Talyonunh took the advice of the Mouse woman by moving on down the river.

It was not very long before he heard scratching under his canoe.

He knew the Otter woman was following him. He tried with all his might to get away from her, but to no avail. She always kept out of sight so that Yobaghu-Talyonunh could not get a chance to kill her.

To throw her off his track, Yobaghu-Talyonunh portaged his canoe to a lake which he crossed.

By evening, seeing and hearing no signs of his enemy, he killed a beaver to eat and made camp for the night. After skinning the beaver, he flung

the skin into the brush as he had no use for it and
went to sleep.

Waking early in the morning, Yobaghu-
Talyonunh found himself covered with a beauti-
fully tanned beaver skin, and looking about in
wonder he saw the Otter woman asleep close by.

He quickly killed her, and it is said that at her
death there sprang from her the mink, the weasel,
the marten, and the ermine.

These Yobaghu-Talyonunh named and put a
value on their skins so that to this day man hunts
these animals for their valuable hides.

14.

OUTSMARTING SILVER-TIP

AFTER Yobaghu-Talyonunh had killed the Otter woman, he returned to the river which he had left.

Soon he rounded a bend and saw a house just below him. Straight out into the stream from one side of the bank was a fence or fish trap. On the bank outside the house, a mouse woman was motioning him to pass by. He wondered why she did not speak and why she wanted him not to stop, but as he approached the camp he noticed on the fence skeletons of many men.

He immediately hurried on.

Before he had gone far, someone caught the back end of his canoe and pulled it ashore.

Yobaghu-Talyonunh soon discovered that he had been made prisoner by the Silver-tip bear man. An enemy of mankind, he used to eat the men that he captured.

Yobaghu-Talyonunh resigned himself to his fate for the time being, as the Silver-tip had decided to keep him prisoner.

To pass the time, Yobaghu-Talyonunh made arrows.

Now, for arrows, one must have pitch, feathers,

and sinew, so one day he said to Silver-tip, "My friend, where do you get your sinew for arrows?"

"Way over on the big flats to the east," replied Silver-tip. "I always get what sinew I need there."

Yobaghu-Talyonunh took his quiver and bow and started.

As he approached the flat, he saw what looked like a great mound. Soon he saw that it was a great serpent. He watched which way the wind blew and kept to the leeward. He could not tell which was the vital part of the beast, and was at a loss to know how to attack.

As he sat wondering, a Mouse came by.

"My friend, help me," he called. "Go find where the heart of yonder thing lies, and I will repay you. Pull all the hair from around the spot and that will serve me as a mark."

The Mouse went off and came to the Serpent.

After locating the place where he could feel the heart beating, he fell to work gnawing off the hair.

The Serpent moved. "What is this I feel about me?" he hissed.

"Oh, I'm just gathering a little fur to keep my children's feet warm," said the Mouse.

After he had made a fine visible target he ran off.

Yobaghu-Talyonunh's aim was sure. The Serpent gave a great leap and lay still. He was dead.

Yobaghu-Talyonunh then went to the Serpent and pulled the required sinews out of the back.

He then returned to Silver-tip.

"Hum. He brought them home," thought the Silver-tip.

The next day Yobaghu-Talyonunh asked where he could get some pitch.

"Down towards the south, beyond those spruce," said Silver-tip.

Yobaghu-Talyonunh went to the south and saw a tree in the distance which seemed to have what he needed.

As he came nearer, he saw that the whole was a live mass of boiling pitch. If any man touched it, he would be dead.

He shot the pitch with arrows, but they only stuck.

Then he got an idea. He gathered thick branches of pitch. He found that when the pitch came in contact with the cold wet branches, it hardened and broke off.

He gathered what he wanted and went home.

"Hum. He has brought it home," thought Silver tip. Yobaghu-Talyonunh was a little too smart.

"If you want feathers, " said Silver-tip, "to the North is where I get mine."

So the next day Yobaghu-Talyonunh started in quest of feathers.

Up on a great rock he could see an Eagle's nest. The birds were nowhere in sight, so he climbed up and found two young ones waiting for their mother and father.

"Where are your father and mother?" he asked.

The baby birds said they had gone off a long time ago and had not returned.

"Who will tell on me when they return?" Yobaghu-Talyonunh asked.

"I will," said the elder.

"How about you?" he asked the younger.

"I will say nothing," he answered.

Yobaghu-Talyonunh took the older bird and threw him over the cliff.

Then he asked for the signs of the parents' returning.

The little bird said that sleet always preceded the mother and hail the father.

Yobaghu-Talyonunh told the little bird not to tell his parents that he had been there and to say that his brother had fallen over the cliff in his sleep.

Yobaghu-Talyonunh went and hid himself behind a rock.

It wasn't long before it began to sleet. The mother bird appeared, holding in her talons the body of a man.

"Where is your brother?" she asked.

"He fell over the cliff in his sleep," said the little eagle.

"What is this I smell?" she asked.

"It must be that which you are carrying," the little bird replied.

As she lifted her head to look around,

Yobaghu-Talyonunh, whose aim was true, struck her with an arrow and she fell over the cliff.

Then it began to hail, and the father bird appeared, carrying in his talons the body of a man.

"Where is your mother?" he demanded.

"She flew past me," said the little one.

"Where is your brother?"

"He fell over the cliff in his sleep."

"What is this I smell?"

As he raised his head to look around, Yobaghu-Talyonunh aimed true, and the father eagle fell off the cliff and rolled to the bottom.

Then Yobaghu-Talyonunh went up to the lonely little bird and told him that what his parents had brought was not fit to eat.

"Wait, I will get you something."

He went up the hill and killed ptarmigan, mountain squirrels, and young lambs. He brought them back to the nest and made the eagle promise that when he was strong enough to hunt for himself he would eat nothing else.

The little bird kept the promise, and to this day eagles still keep that promise.

Yobaghu-Talyonunh gathered some feathers from the big birds and returned to the bear.

"Hum. He has brought them home," Silver-tip said to himself.

The Bear was beginning to get impatient to eat his prisoner, so he asked his two daughters to put on the bear skins and walk around the berry patch on the mountainside.

That day Yobaghu-Talyonunh wanted to hunt, and it was not long before he saw the two bears.

He asked Silver-tip to let him have his arrows, and Silver-tip substituted wild rhubarb arrows for the new ones, thinking he would have Yobaghu-Talyonunh at his mercy later on.

But Yobaghu-Talyonunh had hidden in the back of his garment two good arrows in case of some emergency.

He started after the bears. Finding only the rhubarb arrows in the quiver, he used his two good arrows to kill the two bears.

Silver-tip had thought that with the aid of his two daughters and with Yobaghu-Talyonunh having no arrows, he could kill him easily. But now he found he had to deal with Yobaghu-Talyonunh alone.

When Yobaghu-Talyonunh found that he had nothing with which to protect himself, he started to run through water to throw off the scent from Silver-tip. But he could not get away from him.

At last, growing tired, he dove into a lake. Breaking off one of the big hollow reeds in the lake and letting one end extend out above the water, he was able to remain under the water and breathe.

Silver-tip could not find him.

As he stood peering in the water, he saw a Frog and gruffly asked the Frog to drink up all the water. The Frog began to drink and drink, and grew larger and larger, and the lake began to disappear.

Yobaghu-Talyonunh did not know what to do, but soon a little Sandpiper came by and he asked him if he would go and puncture the Frog.

The little Sandpiper teetered impudently back and forth and said, "Anah," which means "I don't want to."

Then Yobaghu-Talyonunh promised to give the Sandpiper a bead necklace if he would. That is how that white collar came to be around the Sandpiper's neck

The Sandpiper said he would try and went pecking along nearer and nearer the Frog.

"What are you doing?" asked the Frog.

"I'm getting some little things for my children to eat," he said.

When he came close to the Frog, he threw back his head and thrust his beak as far into the Frog as he could, and the water rushed back into the lake.

Silver-tip rushed to the lowest end of the lake and started to tear up the ground to make an outlet to drain the lake. At the head of his outlet he set a trap. He stood and watched so that he could see Yobaghu-Talyonunh if he tried to climb out of the lake. If he tried to swim under the water through the outlet, he would be caught by the trap.

Yobaghu-Talyonunh realized he couldn't get out onto the land so he got as near the trap as he could by swimming under the water. As he was waiting and planning, the Mouse came near him on the bank.

He asked the Mouse to pluck him some hay.

Yobaghu-Talyonunh tied the hay in a big wad and put it on the end of a pole. Pushing this ahead of him, he swam under the water towards the trap. When he came near enough, he pushed the hay into the trap.

Silver-tip thought he had Yobaghu-Talyonunh. He shouted triumphantly and started pulling out his trap.

Yobaghu-Talyonunh slipped under and away, and Silver-tip was much chagrined at finding nothing but the hay in his trap.

Yobaghu-Talyonunh ran quickly through the brush until he came to a swift river which he couldn't cross. He saw a Fox running on the other side, and called to him for help.

The Fox extended his tail across the river, and Yobaghu-Talyonunh crossed on it safely.

"My friend, when the Bear comes to the other bank, put your tail over for him to cross on, and when he is half way over, move your tail so he will fall into the middle of the river. He will soon be here as he is following me."

The Fox waited, and soon the Bear came and called to the Fox for help, and the Fox did what Yobaghu-Talyonunh had told him to do. The Bear was half way over when the Fox moved his tail, and Silver-tip fell into the river.

Yobaghu-Talyonunh escaped while the Bear was getting out of the river.

Yobaghu-Talyonunh had not gone very far after

escaping from Silver-tip when he heard someone calling him. It was a spirit voice saying that something was following him.

He looked back and saw a Bear!

He hid until the Bear came close to try to attack him.

Then Yobaghu-Talyonunh jumped between two trees that were growing very close together. The Bear tried to follow, but he was too big to squeeze through, and Yobaghu-Talyonunh struck him with his club and killed him.

It was a black bear.

To this day the Indians have no fear of black bears, but the Silver-tip is much dreaded.

15.

YOBAGHU-TALYONUNH'S HOMECOMING

YOBAGHU-TALYONUNH began to think about his home. It was wintertime again, and he realized that he could not return to his home by following the horizon. He was at a great loss to know what to do. All the time that he had been traveling he had not met human beings.

One version of the story tells about Yobaghu-Talyonunh's meeting some terrible-looking creatures who resembled human beings in that they had a language and used spears. But they were hostile to him and he had a hard time escaping from them.

This same version related that during this period of his wanderings he met an angel in his sloop who planted a rod of shining metal before him, saying that he was to follow the direction in which the rod lay when he awoke, and that it would eventually bring him to his home.

This version is probably not a part of the original Indian story. It has too much the flavor of a fairy tale and may be of Russian origin.

However he managed to find his way home — for the stories are very vague about it — he at last heard dogs barking in the distance.

Yobaghu-Talyonunh hurried in the direction of the dogs and soon saw that they had cornered a moose.

As he looked over the rolling country, he saw someone running toward him.

He had made some more arrows since he had escaped Silver-tip, and with one of these he shot the moose and let it lie. Then he hid himself and watched to see what the person would do.

He saw more men coming. They were human beings, the first he had seen since he left home. He heard them talking in his own language.

The first runner reached the moose and exclaimed, "How did this happen? The moose is shot with an arrow!"

The others were speechless. The speaker was the oldest among them, and his hair was turning grey.

He examined the arrow very carefully and suddenly, addressing himself to the others, said: "How comes it that this arrow should be here? I know of only one person who feathers an arrow such as this and that is my father."

He was much perplexed because he thought his father was dead long ago.

Yobaghu-Talyonunh was surprised and delighted. He came forward and addressed them, telling them who he was.

It is said that each one in turn clasped their father about the neck, and then they all went home.

When he came into the skin hut where his first wife was, he saw that she had become quite old and that her hair was shaven close.

It has been the custom since then for widows in mourning to cut their hair.

So ends the tale of Yobaghu-Talyonunh. He related his stories to his children and since then they have been handed down in the same way from generations untold.

AFTERWORD

THE year was 1886, and vague rumors began drifting from the North. Rumors of gold fields, rich beyond belief. Gradually men began tracking the rumors and such a man was Henry (Hank) Wright. He traveled to Juneau and Dyea, and then further on into the interior of Alaska. At Tanana, Alaska, he met and married Annie Glass, an Athabascan Indian girl. Henry wintered near Tanana and mined the creeks along the Yukon River. On October 26, 1890, at Old Station, the couple had a son they named Arthur.

In the spring of 1892, five years before the Klondike strike, Henry Wright packed his poke of gold and decided to return "outside." He took his son Arthur and left him with the Rev. Jules Prevost, head of the Episcopal Mission at Tanana. Henry Wright never returned.

Arthur R. Wright was brought up in two cultures, the white man's and the Indian's. He spoke Athabascan, and as a youngster assisted Rev. Prevost in translating a hymnal and a prayer book into Athabascan.

At sixteen, he was sent to St. Matthews Military

Academy in San Mateo, California. He attended for approximately one year.

When he returned to Alaska, he traveled with Archdeacon Hudson Stuck as attendant and interpreter. During their winter travels by dog sled, after the dogs were fed and bedded down, the Archdeacon would read from one of the classics he carried with him. The two men discussed these literary works by campfire on long, cold winter nights.

Arthur studied agriculture at Mt. Herman, Massachusetts, for about three years and then carpentry at a trade school in Philadelphia.

When he returned in 1914, he was put in charge of the boys' work and agriculture at St. Mark's Mission in Nenana for five years.

Then he went on furlough with Bishop Peter Trimble Rowe on a mission fund-raising effort. Later, in Seattle, he attended school to learn to operate a wireless to help connect the missions, but that plan never materialized.

On June 6, 1922, he was ordained as deacon in the Episcopal Church at Nenana.

That same year in Seattle he married Myrtle Rose, a missionary nurse he had known in Nenana who was doing private nursing in Boise, Idaho. Bishop Rowe performed the ceremony.

When Arthur, Myrtle, and Bishop Rowe reached Nenana, they traveled on the *Pelican II*, touring all the missions and villages along the river.

Arthur Wright (behind monument) with Archdeacon Stuck at
the Alaska-Yukon border

When the trio returned to Nenana in mid-
August, the Wrights were sent to Tanana Crossing,
where they spent the next five years operating the
mission before it was closed down for lack of
funds.

The couple spent four years in Nenana, three in Minto, and then returned to Nenana. Here, in 1935, they resigned from the mission work. They had seven sons by then and operated a transfer business in Nenana until Arthur's death in January, 1948.

While Arthur was in service with the Episcopal Church, he translated some Indian folklore into English. He made the translation of the story in this book while at Tanana Crossing, probably in 1924 or 1925. He subsequently published it in the *Alaskan Churchman* in four installments.

JOAN E. WEIS